ORCAS

by **Elizabeth R. Johnson**

Consultant:
Jody Rake, Member,

Southwest Marine Educators Association

CAPSTONE PRESS
a capstone imprint

Pebble Plus is published by Capstone Press,
1710 Roe Crest Drive, North Mankato, Minnesota 56003
www.mycapstone.com

Library of Congress Cataloging-in-Publication Data
Names: Johnson, Elizabeth R., 1986–author.
Title: Orcas / by Elizabeth R. Johnson.
Other titles: Pebble plus. Sea life.
Description: North Mankato, Minnesota : Capstone Press, [2017] | Series:
   Pebble plus. Sea life | Audience: Ages 4–8. | Audience: K to grade 3. |
   Includes bibliographical references and index.
Identifiers: LCCN 2016005489 | ISBN 9781515720799 (library binding) | ISBN
   9781515720836 (eBook PDF)
Subjects: LCSH: Killer whale—Juvenile literature.
Classification: LCC QL737.C432 J63 2017 | DDC 599.53/6—dc23
LC record available at http://lccn.loc.gov/2016005489

Editorial Credits
Jaclyn Jaycox, editor; Philippa Jenkins, designer;
Svetlana Zhurkin, media researcher; Gene Bentdahl, production specialist

Photo Credits
iStockphoto: CostinT, 13, Lazareva, 7, Serega, 17; Newscom: VWPics/Francois Gohier, 15, VWPics/Gerard Lacz, cover, 19, 21; Shutterstock: Mike Price, 3, Miles Away Photography, 11, Monika Wieland, 9, Tory Kallman, 5, Triduza Studio, back cover, 6, 12, 16, 24

Design Elements by Shutterstock

Note to Parents and Teachers

The Sea Life set supports national science standards related to life science. This book describes and illustrates orcas. The images support early readers in understanding the text. The repetition of words and phrases helps early readers learn new words. This book also introduces early readers to subject-specific vocabulary words, which are defined in the Glossary section. Early readers may need assistance to read some words and to use the Table of Contents, Glossary, Read More, Internet Sites, and Index sections of the book.

Printed in China.
022016   007718

Table of Contents

Life in the Ocean

A black and white orca cuts through the waves. Orcas are also called killer whales. They are the largest type of dolphin.

Orcas live in oceans around
the world. They spend their
whole lives in family groups
called pods.

Up Close

An orca's black and white skin acts as camouflage. Orcas are about 22 feet (6.7 meters) long. They weigh as much as 6 tons (5.4 metric tons).

An orca has flukes and flippers.

They help an orca to swim.

An orca also has a tall

dorsal fin.

dorsal fin

flippers

flukes

Orcas love to make noise!
Each pod sounds unique.
An orca can hear its pod
from miles away.

Finding Food

Orcas are one of the world's top predators. Each pod hunts as a team. Orcas eat sea lions and fish. Some pods even hunt sharks and blue whales!

Orcas have about 50 teeth.

The teeth are shaped like cones.

Orcas use their big teeth to

bite and tear prey.

Life Cycle

A baby orca is called a calf.
A newborn calf can be 8.5 feet
(2.6 m) long. It weighs almost
400 pounds (180 kilograms).

Many calves live with their
mothers for their whole lives.
The pod teaches calves
how to hunt and stay safe.
Orcas live about 50 years.

Glossary

calf—a young orca

camouflage—a pattern or color on an animal's skin that helps it blend in with things around it

dorsal fin—a fin located on the back of a dolphin or whale

flipper—one of the broad, flat limbs of a dolphin or whale that help it swim

fluke—part of the tail of a whale or dolphin

pod—a group of whales; pods range from less than five whales to more than 30 whales

predator—an animal that hunts other animals for food; killer whales are top predators because no animals hunt them for food

prey—an animal hunted by another animal for food

unique—one of a kind

Read More

Batten, Mary. *Baby Orca.* New York: Grosset & Dunlap, 2016.

Simon, Charnan. *Killer Whales.* Nature's Children. New York: Children's Press, 2013.

Throp, Claire. *Orcas.* Living in the Wild: Sea Mammals. Chicago, Ill.: Capstone Heinemann Library, 2013.

Internet Sites

FactHound offers a safe, fun way to find Internet sites related to this book. All of the sites on FactHound have been researched by our staff.

Here's all you do:

Visit *www.facthound.com*

Type in this code: 9781515720799

Check out projects, games and lots more at www.capstonekids.com

Index